D1608681

# WHY WE EXERCISE

by Rosalyn Clark

BUMBA BOOKS™

LERNER PUBLICATIONS ◆ MINNEAPOLIS

**Note to Educators:**

Throughout this book, you'll find critical thinking questions. These can be used to engage young readers in thinking critically about the topic and in using the text and photos to do so.

Reader

Lerner Publications Company
A division of Lerner Publishing Group, Inc.
241 First Avenue North
Minneapolis, MN 55401 USA

For reading levels and more information, look up this title at www.lernerbooks.com.

**Library of Congress Cataloging-in-Publication Data**

Names: Clark, Rosalyn, 1990– author.
Title: Why we exercise / Rosalyn Clark.
Description: Minneapolis : Lerner Publications, [2018] | Series: Bumba Books
  — Health Matters | Includes bibliographical references and index. |
  Audience: Ages: 4–7. | Audience: Grades: K to Grade 3.
Identifiers: LCCN 2017019221 (print) | LCCN 2017028838 (ebook) | ISBN
  9781512482973 (eb pdf) | ISBN 9781512482959 (library binding : alk. paper)
  | ISBN 9781541511071 (paperback : alk. paper)
Subjects: LCSH: Exercise—Juvenile literature. | Physical fitness—Juvenile
  literature.
Classification: LCC GV481 (ebook) | LCC GV481 .C6285 2018 (print) | DDC
  613.7/1—dc23

LC record available at https://lccn.loc.gov/2017019221

Manufactured in the United States of America
1 – CG – 12/31/17

Expand learning beyond the printed book. Download free, complementary educational resources for this book from our website, www.lerneresource.com.

# Table of
# Contents

# Let's Move!

It is time to get moving!

How will you exercise today?

There are many ways to exercise.

Climbing at the playground is exercise.

Playing a sport is exercise.

Exercising with others is fun!

**Can you name some sports that are great exercise?**

You can exercise on your own too.

Jumping rope makes your heart

beat fast.

Then your heart moves blood quickly

through your body.

Exercise makes your body strong.

Your muscles work hard.

Your bones grow stronger.

**Why do you think it is important for your bones to be strong?**

Exercise stretches muscles.

It keeps us flexible.

Can you touch your toes?

**Can you think of other ways to stretch your muscles?**

Exercise makes you feel good too.

Being active can make you feel happy!

Exercise even works your brain.

It helps us think more clearly.

It helps us sleep better at night.

Move your body every day.

There are many fun

activities you can try!

# Exercise Gear

**jungle gym**

**water bottle**

**jump rope**

**bicycle**

**tennis shoes**

# Picture Glossary

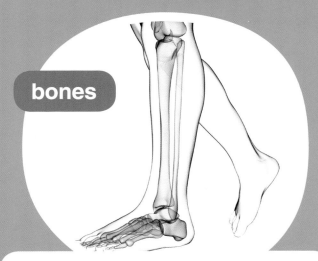

**bones**

hard parts inside your body that make up your skeleton

**flexible**

able to bend and move easily

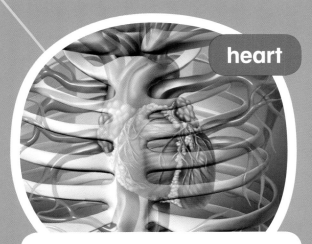

**heart**

the organ in your chest that pumps blood throughout your body

**muscles**

tissues in the body that connect to your bones and make them move

23

# Read More

Bellisario, Gina. *Move Your Body! My Exercise Tips.* Minneapolis: Millbrook Press, 2014.

Black, Vanessa. *Exercise.* Minneapolis: Jump!, 2017.

Morgan, Sally. *How Do We Move?* Mankato, MN: QEB Publishing, 2015.

# Index

## Photo Credits